BIBLEFY

BIBLEFY

AMY SHIELS

TUCKER

DS

PRESS

Published in the USA by Tucker DS Press
Columbus, Ohio

Contact Information
Email: TuckerDSPress@gmail.com
Website: TuckerDSPress.com
Twitter: @FMPBooks
Instagram: @Fayettevillemafiapress
ISBN: 9781959748205
eBook ISBN: 9781959748212

CONTENTS

Dedicated to:

"To Charlie, for teaching me how to love with gratitude and empathy.

And to Cora for teaching me that "every day in every way we can get better and better."

Introduction

"*You might have heard that loud bang just there. That was the engine on the right-hand side of the plane going on fire. We do have another engine that is working; however, we are going to have to make an emergency landing. Unfortunately, we have a full tank of fuel, so we will have to dump that before making the emergency landing or the plane could explode upon impact.*"

These were the words I heard mere moments after takeoff, transmitted over the intercom of a Los Angeles-bound flight from Dublin Airport, Ireland, by our rather charming pilot.

Our Airbus 330 plane, filled to the brim with 262 passengers and eleven crew members, had gone on fire mid-takeoff.

The plane would have to make an "overweight" landing; it would appear nothing is immune to that pesky Christmas-week weight gain.

My immediate reaction: "Let go and let God."

Thirty minutes later, we arrived safely at Shannon Airport. While no injuries were reported, I can only imagine there were a few new believers of a Higher Power.

The Bible is filled with myriad words of wisdom, stories of survival, and examples of being of service to others. Similar to a catchy tune with lyrics that pop into your head every so often, the aforementioned gifts from the Bible are there to help us navigate the world in times of good, bad, and challenge.

I have explored the Books of the Bible multiple times, extracting what I believe to be profound messages and molding them into simple daily mantras. These mantras can serve as sources of inspiration, motivation, comfort, and calm, depending on how you choose to engage with them. *Biblefy* allows you to experience the Bible's teachings in whichever way resonates with you. *Biblefy* is the Bible For You.

I say "Today's Word Today" because older versions of the Bible were extremely violent, and people were raised to be God-fearing. I believe today we know to translate those stories and terms to lean on God loving: being kind to one another and showing care to ourselves. All God's children, every one of us: forgiveness and acceptance of both ourselves and others lead to true freedom for us all.

For those of you who love *Biblefy* and to those of you who don't—I send love to you all.

Warmest,
Amy Shiels

BIBLEFY

AMY SHIELS

JANUARY

TODAY'S WORD TODAY

BIBLEFY

AMY SHIELS

JANUARY 1 2025

"THANK YOU GOD FOR ALL THE BLESSINGS I HAVE HEARD AND SEEN AS YOU WANTED ME TO."

TODAY'S WORD TODAY

BIBLEFY

AMY SHIELS

JANUARY 2 2025

"TEACH US YOUR WAYS THAT WE MAY WALK IN YOUR PATH!"

TODAY'S WORD TODAY

BIBLEFY

AMY SHIELS

"HE GIVES ME WISDOM AND UNDERSTANDING, COUNSEL AND MIGHT, KNOWLEDGE AND LOVE OF THE LORD. HIS GIFTS ARE A DELIGHT."

TODAY'S WORD TODAY

BIBLEFY

AMY SHIELS

"THIS IS OUR LORD, WE TRUST IN HIM - HE WILL SAVE US."

TODAY'S WORD TODAY

BIBLEFY

AMY SHIELS

JANUARY 5 2025

"I RISE AND SHINE BECAUSE YOUR LIGHT HAS COME!"

TODAY'S WORD TODAY

BIBLEFY

AMY SHIELS

JANUARY 6 2025

"IN THE PRESENCE OF DAUNTING DANGERS, GOD PROTECTS US."

TODAY'S WORD TODAY

BIBLEFY

AMY SHIELS

JANUARY 7 2025

"LET US LOVE ONE ANOTHER AS GOD LOVES US ALL."

TODAY'S WORD TODAY

BIBLEFY

AMY SHIELS

"GOD LIVES IN ME - HE HAS GIVEN ME HIS SPIRIT. HE IS LOVE, THEREFORE I AM LOVE."

TODAY'S WORD TODAY

BIBLEFY

AMY SHIELS

JANUARY 9 2025

"GOD PROTECTS THOSE WHOM NO ONE ELSE PROTECTS."

TODAY'S WORD TODAY

BIBLEFY

AMY SHIELS

"I HAVE FAITH IN GOD - I CAN CONQUER THE WORLD!"

TODAY'S WORD TODAY

BIBLEFY

AMY SHIELS

JANUARY 11 2025

"WHATEVER WE ASK ACCORDING TO HIS WILL, GOD HEARS US."

TODAY'S WORD TODAY

JANUARY 12 2025

"I AM HIS BELOVED CHILD. WITH ME HE IS ALWAYS PLEASED."

TODAY'S WORD TODAY

BIBLEFY

AMY SHIELS

JANUARY 13 2025

"I AM BLESSED BECAUSE I DO THE RIGHT THING AND LIVE BY THE LAWS OF OUR GOD."

TODAY'S WORD TODAY

BIBLEFY

AMY SHIELS

JANUARY 14 2025

"I KEEP STRONG IN MY FAITH. MY GOODNESS WILL SHINE THROUGH."

TODAY'S WORD TODAY

BIBLEFY

AMY SHIELS

JANUARY 15 2025

"WHERE GOODNESS IS PREACHED, BADNESS WILL BE PUSHED OUT. I WILL STAY KIND."

TODAY'S WORD TODAY

BIBLEFY

AMY SHIELS

JANUARY 16 2025

"I TRUST IN MY FAITH AND WILL LEAN ON HIM UNTIL THE VERY END!"

TODAY'S WORD TODAY

BIBLEFY

AMY SHIELS

JANUARY 17 2025

"NOTHING IS HIDDEN FROM GOD'S SIGHT. HE SEES THE GOOD I DO."

TODAY'S WORD TODAY

BIBLEFY

AMY SHIELS

JANUARY 18 2025

"I DO NOT JUDGE THE SINNERS FOR THEY NEED LOVE THE MOST."

TODAY'S WORD TODAY

BIBLEFY

AMY SHIELS

JANUARY 19 2025

"BE FREE AND SERVE THE LORD WITH LOVE."

TODAY'S WORD TODAY

BIBLEFY

AMY SHIELS

JANUARY 20   2025

"BE GENTLE WITH THE IGNORANT AND THE WAYWARD. KINDNESS COMES BACK TO THE SELF."

TODAY'S WORD TODAY

BIBLEFY

AMY SHIELS

JANUARY 21 2025

"GOD IS JUST. HE WILL REMEMBER MY GOOD WORK AND THE LOVE I HAVE SHOWN HIM."

TODAY'S WORD TODAY

BIBLEFY

AMY SHIELS

JANUARY 22 2025

"IF I AM KIND OF HEART AND POSITIVE TO IDEAS. I AM LIGHT AND LOVE"

TODAY'S WORD TODAY

BIBLEFY

AMY SHIELS

JANUARY 23 2025

"I DRAW NEAR TO GOD BECAUSE WITH HIM I AM LOVED."

TODAY'S WORD TODAY

BIBLEFY

AMY SHIELS

JANUARY 24 2025

"WHAT NO LONGER SERVES ME IS READY TO VANISH AWAY."

TODAY'S WORD TODAY

BIBLEFY

AMY SHIELS

JANUARY 25 2025

"I WILL GO INTO THE WORLD AND SHARE. THOSE WHO BELIEVE WILL BE SAVED!"

TODAY'S WORD TODAY

BIBLEFY

AMY SHIELS

JANUARY 26 2025

"LORD, YOU ARE A SHIELD TO ME. HELP LIFT MY SPIRITS UP."

TODAY'S WORD TODAY

BIBLEFY

AMY SHIELS

JANUARY 27 2025

"GOD'S GIFT OF ETERNAL LIFE HAS NO STRINGS ATTACHED."

TODAY'S WORD TODAY

BIBLEFY

AMY SHIELS

"I HAVE COME TO DO YOUR WILL, MY GOD. LEAD ME TO YOUR PATH."

TODAY'S WORD TODAY

BIBLEFY

AMY SHIELS

JANUARY 29 2025

"WHEN SIN HAS BEEN FORGIVEN, SACRIFICE FOR SIN IS NO LONGER NECESSARY. I FREE MYSELF WITH FORGIVENESS."

TODAY'S WORD TODAY

BIBLEFY

AMY SHIELS

JANUARY 30 2025

"I AM A GOOD LISTENER. THE MORE I HEAR THE MORE UNDERSTANDING I WILL BE GIVEN."

TODAY'S WORD TODAY

BIBLEFY

AMY SHIELS

JANUARY 31 2025

"THE JUST LIVE BY FAITH; I WILL BE REWARDED."

TODAY'S WORD TODAY

BIBLEFY
AMY SHIELS

FEBRUARY

TODAY'S WORD TODAY

BIBLEFY

AMY SHIELS

"I HAVE FAITH."

TODAY'S WORD TODAY

BIBLEFY

AMY SHIELS

FEBRUARY 2 2025

"I BELIEVE. THE LORD I AM SEEKING IS ALL AROUND ME."

TODAY'S WORD TODAY

BIBLEFY

AMY SHIELS

FEBRUARY 3 2025

"I AM A LIGHT FOR OTHERS. I SHARE HOW MUCH THE LORD HAS DONE FOR ME. "

TODAY'S WORD TODAY

BIBLEFY

AMY SHIELS

FEBRUARY 4 2025

"I THROW OFF EVERYTHING THAT HINDERS ME! I AM STRONG AND I FOLLOW MY HEART."

TODAY'S WORD TODAY

BIBLEFY

AMY SHIELS

FEBRUARY 5 2025

"I HAVE ENDURED HARDSHIP TO GROW. THE LORD LOVES ME."

TODAY'S WORD TODAY

BIBLEFY

AMY SHIELS

"IF ANY PLACE WILL NOT WELCOME ME, I LEAVE AND SHAKE THE DUST OFF MY FEET. I AM BEAUTIFUL."

TODAY'S WORD TODAY

BIBLEFY

AMY SHIELS

FEBRUARY 7 2025

"BY SHOWING HOSPITALITY TO STRANGERS I MAY UNKNOWINGLY HELP AN ANGEL."

TODAY'S WORD TODAY

BIBLEFY

AMY SHIELS

FEBRUARY 8 2025

"MY MIND IS CLEAR: I APPRECIATE THIS QUIET PLACE FOR SOME REST."

TODAY'S WORD TODAY

BIBLEFY

AMY · SHIELS

FEBRUARY 9 2025

"I AM NOT AFRAID. I AM OF SERVICE TO OTHERS AND THE REST WILL LOOK AFTER ITSELF."

TODAY'S WORD TODAY

BIBLEFY

AMY SHIELS

FEBRUARY 10   2025

"LET THERE BE LIGHT!"

TODAY'S WORD TODAY

BIBLEFY

AMY SHIELS

FEBRUARY 11 2025

"LET US BE FREE!"

TODAY'S WORD TODAY

BIBLEFY

AMY SHIELS

FEBRUARY 12 2025

"I LET GO OF WHAT HURTS ME INSIDE. I BREATHE IN THE GOOD TO CLEAN MY SOUL."

TODAY'S WORD TODAY

BIBLEFY

AMY SHIELS

FEBRUARY 13 2025

"I THROW SHAME AWAY. IT IS USELESS"

TODAY'S WORD TODAY

BIBLEFY

AMY SHIELS

FEBRUARY 14 2025

"I ASK FOR HEALING. HE IS LISTENING."

TODAY'S WORD TODAY

BIBLEFY

AMY SHIELS

FEBRUARY 15 2025

"I HAVE COMPASSION FOR OTHERS - WHATEVER THEY ARE GOING THROUGH."

TODAY'S WORD TODAY

BIBLEFY

AMY SHIELS

FEBRUARY 16 2025

"I HAVE HOPE IN CHRIST, WE ARE ALL LOVED."

TODAY'S WORD TODAY

BIBLEFY

AMY SHIELS

FEBRUARY 17 2025

"I DO WHAT IS RIGHT."

TODAY'S WORD TODAY

BIBLEFY

AMY SHIELS

FEBRUARY 18 2025

"I HAVE PATIENCE THEREFORE I WILL BE GIVEN INSIGHT."

TODAY'S WORD TODAY

BIBLEFY

AMY SHIELS

FEBRUARY 19 2025

A LITTLE FAITH CAN BLOSSOM INTO SOMETHING MUCH GREATER. I KEEP PUSHING FORWARD.

TODAY'S WORD TODAY

BIBLEFY

AMY SHIELS

FEBRUARY 20 2025

"MY GIFTS ARE BOUNTIFUL - I SHARE THEM WITH THE WORLD."

TODAY'S WORD TODAY

BIBLEFY

AMY SHIELS

FEBRUARY 21 2025

"I AM OF SERVICE TO OTHERS, MY LIFE IS FILLED WITH ABUNDANCE."

TODAY'S WORD TODAY

BIBLEFY

AMY SHIELS

FEBRUARY 22 2025

"I HAVE COURAGE AND HOPE IN THE LORD. HE WILL SHARE WITH ME THE KEY TO THE KINGDOM OF HEAVEN"

TODAY'S WORD TODAY

BIBLEFY

AMY SHIELS

FEBRUARY 23 2025

"THE LORD REWARDS OUR RIGHTEOUSNESS AND FAITHFULNESS."

TODAY'S WORD TODAY

BIBLEFY

AMY SHIELS

"EVERYTHING IS POSSIBLE WHEN I BELIEVE."

TODAY'S WORD TODAY

BIBLEFY

AMY SHIELS

FEBRUARY 25 2025

"I AM PATIENT IN CHANGES THAT HUMBLE ME FOR GOLD IS TESTED IN FIRE."

TODAY'S WORD TODAY

BIBLEFY

AMY SHIELS

FEBRUARY 26 2025

"WHOEVER IS NOT AGAINST US IS FOR US."

TODAY'S WORD TODAY

BIBLEFY

AMY SHIELS

FEBRUARY 27 2025

"I HAVE PURITY IN AND PEACE IN MY HEART."

TODAY'S WORD TODAY

BIBLEFY

AMY SHIELS

FEBRUARY 28 2025

"I ALLOW THOSE WHO ARE FRIENDLY WITH ME BE MANY BUT KEEP MY ADVISORS FEW."

TODAY'S WORD TODAY

BIBLEFY

AMY SHIELS

MARCH

TODAY'S WORD TODAY

BIBLEFY

AMY SHIELS

MARCH 1 2025

"WE ARE ALL SINNERS, GOD KNOWS THIS."

TODAY'S WORD TODAY

BIBLEFY

AMY SHIELS

MARCH 2 2025

"I LOVE MY CHALLENGERS AND PRAY FOR THEIR WELL-BEING."

TODAY'S WORD TODAY

BIBLEFY

AMY SHIELS

MARCH 3 2025

"ALL THINGS ARE POSSIBLE WITH GOD."

TODAY'S WORD TODAY

BIBLEFY

AMY SHIELS

MARCH 4 2025

"I AM GENEROUS AND KNOW HE WILL REPAY ME SEVENFOLD."

TODAY'S WORD TODAY

BIBLEFY

AMY SHIELS

MARCH 5 2025

"I HAVE INTEGRITY: GOD, SEES WHAT GOOD I DO IN PRIVATE AND REWARS ME."

TODAY'S WORD TODAY

BIBLEFY

AMY SHIELS

"BY HELPING OTHERS WE SAVE OURSELVES."

TODAY'S WORD TODAY

BIBLEFY

AMY SHIELS

MARCH 7 2025

"I SIT AND PRAY AND THE LORD SHALL ANSWER."

TODAY'S WORD TODAY

BIBLEFY

AMY SHIELS

MARCH 8 2025

"LORD, PLEASE BLESS ME TO RISE ABOVE ALL OBSTACLES."

TODAY'S WORD TODAY

BIBLEFY

AMY SHIELS

MARCH 9 2025

"GOD'S LOVE FOR ME IS LIKE AN ENDURING ROCK: STEADFAST, UNWAVERING AND PERMANENT ."

TODAY'S WORD TODAY

BIBLEFY

AMY SHIELS

MARCH 10 2025

"IN THE LORD'S EYES WE ARE ALL EQUAL. WHEN I HELP OTHERS I AM HELPING HIM."

TODAY'S WORD TODAY

MARCH 11 2025

"I TAKE COMFORT IN KNOWING THAT GOD MEANS WHAT HE SAYS. HE IS FOREVER BY MY SIDE."

TODAY'S WORD TODAY

MARCH 12 2025

"I MAY NOT ALWAYS UNDERSTAND GOD'S PLAN YET WITH FAITH I KNOW IT IS GOOD."

TODAY'S WORD TODAY

BIBLEFY

AMY SHIELS

MARCH 13 2025

"I WILL TRANSFORM MY GRIEF INTO JOY AND MY SADNESS INTO INTEGRITY."

TODAY'S WORD TODAY

BIBLEFY

AMY SHIELS

MARCH 14 2025

"I SETTLE MATTERS SWIFTLY TO GIFT MYSELF WITH FREEDOM."

TODAY'S WORD TODAY

BIBLEFY

AMY SHIELS

MARCH 15 2025

"WHEN I LISTEN TO GOD, HE ELEVATES ME TO FAME AND HONOR ABOVE ALL NATIONS."

TODAY'S WORD TODAY

BIBLEFY

AMY SHIELS

MARCH 16 2025

"YES, HE DEPARTED, BUT HE RETURNED TO BE WITH US FOREVER . . . "

TODAY'S WORD TODAY

BIBLEFY

AMY SHIELS

MARCH 17 2025

"NO MATTER WHAT, GOD HAS MERCY AND FORGIVES ME."

TODAY'S WORD TODAY

BIBLEFY

AMY SHIELS

MARCH 18 2025

"I AM OBEDIENT. HE WILL SHARE THE GOOD THINGS OF THE LAND."

TODAY'S WORD TODAY

BIBLEFY

AMY SHIELS

MARCH 19 2025

"MY DESTINY AND KINGDOM WILL BE SECURED FOREVER THROUGH GOD."

TODAY'S WORD TODAY

BIBLEFY

AMY SHIELS

MARCH 20 2025

"BLESSED AM I WHO TRUSTS IN THE LORD!"

BIBLEFY

AMY SHIELS

MARCH 21 2025

"ALL THINGS WORK TOGETHER FOR GOOD FOR I LOVE THE LORD."

TODAY'S WORD TODAY

BIBLEFY

AMY SHIELS

MARCH 22 2025

"IF I AM LOST I WILL BE FOUND, FOR GOD IS ALWAYS WITH ME."

TODAY'S WORD TODAY

BIBLEFY

AMY SHIELS

MARCH 23 2025

"HEAVEN IS LIKE YEAST MIXED INTO ABOUT SIXTY POUNDS OF FLOUR UNTIL IT IS WORKED ALL THROUGH THE DOUGH."

TODAY'S WORD TODAY

BIBLEFY

AMY SHIELS

MARCH 24 2025

"WE ARE ALL GOD'S CHILDREN. EVERY SINGLE ONE OF US. HE LOVES US ALL."

TODAY'S WORD TODAY

BIBLEFY

"I AM HIGHLY FAVORED. THE LORD IS WITH ME."

TODAY'S WORD TODAY

BIBLEFY

AMY SHIELS

MARCH 26 2025

"I TAKE CARE TO WATCH MY LIFE CLOSELY THAT I MAY SHARE STORIES WITH THE NEXT GENERATION."

TODAY'S WORD TODAY

BIBLEFY

AMY SHIELS

MARCH 27 2025

"WHOEVER IS WITH ME IS FOR ME!"

BIBLEFY

AMY SHIELS

MARCH 28 2025

"WHEN I GIFT LOVE I AM CLOSER TO HEAVEN."

TODAY'S WORD TODAY

BIBLEFY

AMY SHIELS

MARCH 29 2025

"GOD, HAVE MERCY ON ME, A SINNER!"

"I REST EASY; WE ARE ALL SINNERS, GOD LOVES US ALL."

TODAY'S WORD TODAY

BIBLEFY

AMY SHIELS

MARCH 30 2025

"I LIVE AS A CHILD OF LIGHT: SEEKING GOODNESS, CURIOSITY AND TRUTH."

TODAY'S WORD TODAY

BIBLEFY

AMY SHIELS

MARCH 31 2025

"I TAKE MY TIME AND SEE SIGNS AND MIRACLES ALL AROUND ME."

TODAY'S WORD TODAY

BIBLEFY

AMY SHIELS

APRIL

TODAY'S WORD TODAY

BIBLEFY

AMY SHIELS

"I WILL PICK MYSELF UP AND DO THE THING."

TODAY'S WORD TODAY

BIBLEFY

AMY SHIELS

APRIL 2 2025

"I SHOUT FOR JOY: THE LORD COMFORTS AND HAS COMPASSION FOR ME."

TODAY'S WORD TODAY

BIBLEFY

AMY SHIELS

APRIL 3 2025

"GOD IS A LAMP THAT BURNS AND GIVES LIGHT - I WILL BE A BEAM OF HIS BRIGHT LIGHT."

TODAY'S WORD TODAY

BIBLEFY

AMY SHIELS

APRIL 4 2025

"I LOVE YOU LORD. PLEASE HELP ME OUT OF MY TROUBLES."

TODAY'S WORD TODAY

BIBLEFY

AMY SHIELS

"I LISTEN THAT I MAY LEARN."

TODAY'S WORD TODAY

BIBLEFY

AMY SHIELS

APRIL 6 2025

"I PRAY TO GOD THAT HE WILL BRING ME BACK TO JOY."

TODAY'S WORD TODAY

BIBLEFY

AMY SHIELS

APRIL 7 2025

"I LOOK TO HEAVEN AND REMEMBER MY DUTY TO JUSTICE."

TODAY'S WORD TODAY

BIBLEFY

AMY SHIELS

APRIL 8 2025

"GOD IS STEADFAST BY MY SIDE."

TODAY'S WORD TODAY

BIBLEFY

AMY SHIELS

APRIL 9 2025

"GOD WOULD DELIVER ME FROM A BLAZING FURNACE."

TODAY'S WORD TODAY

BIBLEFY

AMY SHIELS

APRIL 10 2025

"GOD GLORIFIES ME. I AM HIS CHILD."

TODAY'S WORD TODAY

BIBLEFY

AMY SHIELS

APRIL 11 2025

"I SING TO THE LORD! HE RESCUES ME."

TODAY'S WORD TODAY

BIBLEFY

AMY SHIELS

APRIL 12 2025

"GOD'S SANCTUARY IS AMONG US FOREVER. I TAKE TIME TO TRULY APPRECIATE IT."

TODAY'S WORD TODAY

BIBLEFY

AMY SHIELS

APRIL 13 2025

"THANK YOU LORD FOR SUSTAINING ME. HE AWAKENS ME EVERY MORING IN MY EARS AND IN MY EYES."

TODAY'S WORD TODAY

BIBLEFY

AMY SHIELS

APRIL 14 2025

"THE LORD WILL TAKE HOLD OF MY HAND AND OPEN MY EYES TO RELEASE ME FROM DARKNES."

TODAY'S WORD TODAY

BIBLEFY

AMY SHIELS

APRIL 15 2025

"THE LORD HAS MADE ME A SHARPENED ARROW, IN HIS QUIVER HE HAS HIDDEN ME."

TODAY'S WORD TODAY

BIBLEFY

AMY SHIELS

"I LISTEN FIRST TO UNDERSTAND WHAT THEY SAY."

TODAY'S WORD TODAY

BIBLEFY

AMY SHIELS

"TODAY IS A NEW DAY - A NEW START ON LIFE!"

TODAY'S WORD TODAY

BIBLEFY

AMY SHIELS

APRIL 18 2025

"I APPROACH GOD'S THRONE OF GRACE WITH CONFIDENCE, SO THAT I MAY FIND GRACE TO HELP ME IN TIME OF NEED."

TODAY'S WORD TODAY

BIBLEFY

AMY SHIELS

APRIL 19 2025

"THE LORD HAS ENDOWED ME WITH SPLENDOR!"

TODAY'S WORD TODAY

BIBLEFY

AMY SHIELS

APRIL 20 2025

"I SET MY MIND ON A HIGHER PURPOSE, NOT ON EARTHLY THINGS."

TODAY'S WORD TODAY

BIBLEFY

AMY SHIELS

APRIL 21 2025

"THE LORD IS AT MY RIGHT HAND, I WILL NOT BE SHAKEN."

TODAY'S WORD TODAY

BIBLEFY

AMY SHIELS

APRIL 22 2025

"I REPENT IN THE NAME OF JESUS CHRIST FOR THE FORGIVENESS OF MY SINS. I WILL RECEIVE THE GIFT OF THE HOLY SPIRIT."

TODAY'S WORD TODAY

BIBLEFY

AMY SHIELS

APRIL 23 2025

"WHAT I DO HAVE IS LOVE AND THAT LOVE I SHARE WITH ABUNDANCE."

TODAY'S WORD TODAY

BIBLEFY

AMY SHIELS

APRIL 24 2025

"DEAR GOD, PLEASE GUIDE ME TOWARDS POSITIVE PATHS AND SURROUND ME WITH POSITIVE PEOPLE."

TODAY'S WORD TODAY

BIBLEFY

AMY SHIELS

APRIL 25 2025

"I CAN AND WILL BE STRONG IN HIS NAME."

TODAY'S WORD TODAY

BIBLEFY

AMY SHIELS

APRIL 26 2025

"I GO INTO THE WORLD TODAY AND SHARE KINDNESS."

TODAY'S WORD TODAY

BIBLEFY

AMY SHIELS

"I AM CONFIDENT AND SHOW OTHERS THEY CAN LEAN ON ME."

TODAY'S WORD TODAY

BIBLEFY

AMY SHIELS

"I AM KIND TO OTHERS AND SHARE REFUGE IN GOD'S LOVE."

TODAY'S WORD TODAY

BIBLEFY

AMY SHIELS

APRIL 29 2025

"I AM A PERSON OF ENCOURAGEMENT!"

TODAY'S WORD TODAY

BIBLEFY

AMY SHIELS

APRIL 30 2025

"I LIVE IN TRUTH THAT I MAY BATHE IN THE LIGHT. LET TODAY BE THE DAY I LIVE TRUTHFULLY."

TODAY'S WORD TODAY

BIBLEFY

AMY SHIELS

MAY

TODAY'S WORD TODAY

BIBLEFY

AMY SHIELS

MAY 1 2025

"I CHOOSE TO LOVE MYSELF, AND ABOVE ALL LIVE WITH LOVE IN MY HEART."

TODAY'S WORD TODAY

BIBLEFY

AMY SHIELS

MAY 2 2025

"GOD HAS THE POWER TO AMPLIFY WHATEVER I CHOOSE TO OFFER."

TODAY'S WORD TODAY

BIBLEFY

AMY SHIELS

MAY 3 2025

"I ACCEPT THIS CHALLENGE BECAUSE I BELIEVE IN THE HOLY SPIRIT, AND PRAY TO HIM FOR HIS GUIDANCE."

TODAY'S WORD TODAY

BIBLEFY

AMY SHIELS

MAY 4 2025

"JESUS BELIEVES IN ME. I WILL GET BACK UP AND TRY AGAIN."

TODAY'S WORD TODAY

MAY 5 2025

"I FOCUS NOT ON PERISHABLE PURSUITS, RATHER ON THAT WHICH SUSTAINS ETERNAL LIFE."

TODAY'S WORD TODAY

BIBLEFY

AMY SHIELS

"I WILL EXAMINE MY HEART AND TRUST IN THE HIGHER POWER."

TODAY'S WORD TODAY

BIBLEFY

AMY SHIELS

MAY 7 2025

"I BELIEVE IN SHOWING KINDNESS TO OTHERS. SMALL ACTS CHANGE THE WORLD."

TODAY'S WORD TODAY

BIBLEFY

AMY SHIELS

MAY 8 2025

"GOD TRANSCENDS HUMAN LIMITATIONS AND BELIEFS. HE SEES WHAT I CAN'T YET SEE."

TODAY'S WORD TODAY

BIBLEFY

AMY SHIELS

MAY 9 2025

"IN ALL THAT I DO I WILL LEAN ON MY FAITH."

TODAY'S WORD TODAY

BIBLEFY

AMY SHIELS

MAY 10 2025

"I WILL FOLLOW THE LORD AND IT WILL BE REWARDING."

TODAY'S WORD TODAY

BIBLEFY

AMY SHIELS

MAY 11 2025

"I KEEP WONDER IN MY HEART AND SEE BLESSINGS BEYOND BELIEF."

TODAY'S WORD TODAY

BIBLEFY

AMY SHIELS

MAY 12 2025

"NO MATTER WHAT I DO OR WHERE I GO - GOD STAYS BY MY SIDE."

TODAY'S WORD TODAY

BIBLEFY

AMY SHIELS

MAY 13 2025

"I TAKE TIME TO FEEL THE GRACE OF GOD WITHIN ME AND SHARE HIS BLESSINGS."

TODAY'S WORD TODAY

BIBLEFY

AMY SHIELS

MAY 14 2025

"HIS JOY LIVES IN ME. I AM COMPLETE."

TODAY'S WORD TODAY

BIBLEFY

AMY SHIELS

MAY 15 2025

"WHOEVER WELCOMES ANYONE HE SENDS IS ALSO WELCOMING HIM."

TODAY'S WORD TODAY

BIBLEFY

AMY SHIELS

MAY 16 2025

"I DO NOT LET MY HEART BE TROUBLED. I SHARE MY WORRIES WITH GOD WHO LOVES ME."

TODAY'S WORD TODAY

BIBLEFY

AMY SHIELS

MAY 17 2025

"I LEAN IN AND LOVE GOD DEEPLY."

TODAY'S WORD TODAY

BIBLEFY

AMY SHIELS

MAY 18 2025

"I LOVE OTHES AS GOD HAS LOVED ME WITH PATIENCE AND GRACE."

TODAY'S WORD TODAY

BIBLEFY

AMY SHIELS

MAY 19 2025

"ALL OF MY ACTIONS ARE GUIDED BY A DEEP LOVE FOR GOD."

TODAY'S WORD TODAY

BIBLEFY

AMY SHIELS

MAY 20 2025

"MY HEART IS STRONG - I AM CONFIDENT."

TODAY'S WORD TODAY

BIBLEFY

AMY SHIELS

MAY 21 2025

"I WILL BELIEVE IN ME LIKE I BELIEVE IN YOU."

TODAY'S WORD TODAY

BIBLEFY

AMY SHIELS

MAY 22 2025

"I PRAY TO BE AS JESUS WAS: FULL OF LOVE AND KINDNESS."

TODAY'S WORD TODAY

BIBLEFY

AMY SHIELS

MAY 23 2025

"I ACCEPT PEOPLE FOR WHO THEY ARE AND WHERE THEY ARE."

TODAY'S WORD TODAY

BIBLEFY

AMY SHIELS

MAY 24 2025

"I EXPERIENCE JOY WHERE I CAN AND LOOK FOR THE GOOD, ALWAYS."

TODAY'S WORD TODAY

BIBLEFY

AMY SHIELS

MAY 25 2025

"I WILL NOT LET MY HEART BE TROUBLED. HE WILL SHOW ME THE ROUTE TO TAKE."

TODAY'S WORD TODAY

BIBLEFY

AMY SHIELS

MAY 26 2025

"GOD OFFERS SALVATION TO US ALL."

TODAY'S WORD TODAY

BIBLEFY

AMY SHIELS

MAY 27 2025

"I AM STRONG, AND I AM LOVED."

TODAY'S WORD TODAY

BIBLEFY

AMY SHIELS

MAY 28 2025

"THERE ARE SO MANY THINGS TO LEARN; HE WILL TEACH ME IN GOOD TIME."

TODAY'S WORD TODAY

MAY 29 2025

"MAY GOD GIVE ME THE GIFT OF UNDERSTANDING, EMPATHY, AND ENLIGHTENMENT."

TODAY'S WORD TODAY

BIBLEFY

AMY SHIELS

MAY 30 2025

"I DO THE RIGHT THING BECAUSE GOD IS WITH ME."

TODAY'S WORD TODAY

BIBLEFY

AMY SHIELS

MAY 31 2025

"LET MY SOUL MAGNIFY AND REJOICE IN THE LORD."

TODAY'S WORD TODAY

BIBLEFY

AMY SHIELS

JUNE

TODAY'S WORD TODAY

BIBLEFY

AMY SHIELS

JUNE 1 2025

"I PRAY FOR WISDOM TO UNDERSTAND MY PURPOSE AND FEEL YOUR RICHES ON EARTH."

TODAY'S WORD TODAY

BIBLEFY

AMY SHIELS

JUNE 2 2025

"WHEN I FACE CHALLENGES I STAY STRONG BECAUSE THE LORD IS ALWAYS WITH ME."

TODAY'S WORD TODAY

BIBLEFY

AMY SHIELS

JUNE 3 2025

"THANK YOU GOD, FOR YOUR SUPPORT."

BIBLEFY

AMY SHIELS

JUNE 4 2025

"IT IS MY DUTY TO BE OF SERVICE TO OTHERS."

TODAY'S WORD TODAY

BIBLEFY

AMY SHIELS

JUNE 5 2025

"GOD WANTS US TO UNITE AS A COMMUNITY AND SPREAD KINDNESS WHEREVER WE GO."

TODAY'S WORD TODAY

BIBLEFY

AMY SHIELS

JUNE 6 2025

"I RESPECT GOD BY NOT JUDGING OTHERS."

TODAY'S WORD TODAY

BIBLEFY

AMY SHIELS

JUNE 7 2025

"I FOCUS ON MY OWN ISSUES AND STAY OUT OF OTHERS' AFFAIRS."

TODAY'S WORD TODAY

BIBLEFY

AMY SHIELS

JUNE 8 2025

"THE EXPRESSION OF THE SPIRIT IS BESTOWED UPON ME EVERY DAY."

TODAY'S WORD TODAY

BIBLEFY

AMY SHIELS

JUNE 9 2025

"I SHARE MY KINDNESS WITH OTHERS FOR THE GREATER GOOD."

TODAY'S WORD TODAY

JUNE 10 2025

"I TRUST YOU GOD FOR YOU ALWAYS FULFILL YOUR PROMISES."

TODAY'S WORD TODAY

BIBLEFY

AMY SHIELS

JUNE 11 2025

"I FEEL THE GRACE OF GOD - I AM FOREVER FAITHFUL!"

TODAY'S WORD TODAY

BIBLEFY

AMY SHIELS

JUNE 12 2025

"WHEREVER THE LORD'S PRESENCE IS EXPERIENCED, FREEDOM FLOURISHES."

TODAY'S WORD TODAY

BIBLEFY

AMY SHIELS

JUNE 13 2025

"I MIGHT FACE PERSECUTION, BUT I WILL NEVER BE ABANDONED."

TODAY'S WORD TODAY

BIBLEFY

AMY SHIELS

"IN CHRIST I AM AN EVER CHANGING CREATION; THE OLD HAS GONE, AND THE NEW HAS COME!"

TODAY'S WORD TODAY

BIBLEFY

AMY SHIELS

JUNE 15 2025

"I HAVE FAITH, I HAVE PATIENCE, I HAVE PEACE, I HAVE HOPE."

TODAY'S WORD TODAY

BIBLEFY

AMY SHIELS

JUNE 16 2025

"I WORK FOR THE GRACE OF GOD, AND I AM TRULY THANKFUL FOR IT."

TODAY'S WORD TODAY

BIBLEFY

AMY SHIELS

JUNE 17 2025

"I EXCEL IN ALL THINGS—FAITH, KNOWLEDGE, DILIGENCE, AND LOVE—I WILL WORK TO EXCEL IN THIS GRACE."

TODAY'S WORD TODAY

BIBLEFY

AMY SHIELS

JUNE 18 2025

"I PRACTICE MY FAITH QUIETLY, SINCERELY AND WITH GRACE."

TODAY'S WORD TODAY

JUNE 19 2025

"IF I MUST SEEK GLORY, LET IT BE IN RELATION TO MY WEAKNESSES."

TODAY'S WORD TODAY

BIBLEFY

AMY SHIELS

JUNE 20 2025

"I WORK DILIGENTLY TO DO THE RIGHT THING TO FULFILL GOD'S WISHES."

TODAY'S WORD TODAY

BIBLEFY

AMY SHIELS

JUNE 21 2025

"MY STRENGTH IS MADE PERFECT IN WEAKNESS."

TODAY'S WORD TODAY

BIBLEFY

AMY SHIELS

"I AM GRATEFUL FOR THE FOOD I AM ABOUT TO EAT."

TODAY'S WORD TODAY

JUNE 23 2025

"I WILL NOT JUDGE OR I TOO SHALL BE JUDGED."

TODAY'S WORD TODAY

BIBLEFY

AMY SHIELS

JUNE 24 2025

"I AM NOT AFRAID. MY PRAYER WILL BE HEARD."

TODAY'S WORD TODAY

BIBLEFY

AMY SHIELS

JUNE 25 2025

"I AM BRAVE BECAUSE GOD IS MY SHIELD."

TODAY'S WORD TODAY

BIBLEFY

AMY SHIELS

JUNE 26 2025

"GOD DOES NOT OPERATE ON OUR SCHEDULE; HE MOVES IN HIS OWN TIME."

TODAY'S WORD TODAY

JUNE 27 2025

"I TAKE RESPONSIBILITY FOR MY LIFE AND CONSIDER MY IMPACT ON OTHERS."

TODAY'S WORD TODAY

BIBLEFY

AMY SHIELS

JUNE 28 2025

"I FOLLOW YOUR PATH WHEREVER IT MAY LEAD AND KNOW YOU WILL HELP ME, LORD."

TODAY'S WORD TODAY

BIBLEFY

AMY SHIELS

JUNE 29 2025

"THE LORD SENDS ANGELS TO PROTECT ME."

TODAY'S WORD TODAY

BIBLEFY

AMY SHIELS

JUNE 30 2025

"LORD, I WILL FOLLOW YOU. PLEASE GUIDE ME ON THE PATH I SHOULD TAKE."

TODAY'S WORD TODAY

BIBLEFY

AMY SHIELS

JULY

TODAY'S WORD TODAY

BIBLEFY

AMY SHIELS

JULY 1 2025

"I AM NOT FEARFUL FOR I HAVE STRONG FAITH."

TODAY'S WORD TODAY

BIBLEFY

AMY SHIELS

JULY 2 2025

"WE ARE ALL GOD'S CHILDREN. EVERY SINGLE ONE."

TODAY'S WORD TODAY

BIBLEFY

AMY SHIELS

JULY 3 2025

"NONE OF US ARE STRANGERS; WE ARE FELLOW CITIZENS WITH THE SAINTS AND GOD'S HOUSEHOLD MEMBERS."

TODAY'S WORD TODAY

BIBLEFY

AMY SHIELS

JULY 4 2025

"I AM MERCIFUL TO OTHERS AS GOD IS MERCIFUL TO ME."

TODAY'S WORD TODAY

BIBLEFY

AMY SHIELS

JULY 5 2025

"GOD TRANSFORMS NEGATIVE EXPERIENCES INTO OPPORTUNITIES FOR POSITIVE OUTCOMES."

TODAY'S WORD TODAY

JULY 6 2025

"THE JOY HE INVITES ME TO EXPERIENCE IS TRUE FULFILLMENT."

TODAY'S WORD TODAY

BIBLEFY

AMY SHIELS

JULY 7 2025

"GOD BE WITH ME AND WATCH OVER ME ON THIS JOURNEY I AM TAKING."

TODAY'S WORD TODAY

BIBLEFY

AMY SHIELS

JULY 8 2025

"LORD, PLEASE SHOW ME HOW TO HEAL."

TODAY'S WORD TODAY

BIBLEFY

AMY SHIELS

JULY 9 2025

"THE GOOD WE DO MAY NOT BE IMMEDIATELY REWARDED, BUT IT IS ALWAYS SEEN."

TODAY'S WORD TODAY

BIBLEFY

AMY SHIELS

JULY 10 2025

"WHERE I AM NOT APPRECIATED, AS I LEAVE THAT PLACE, I WILL SHAKE THE DUST OFF MY FEET."

TODAY'S WORD TODAY

BIBLEFY

AMY SHIELS

JULY 11 2025

"I AM CONFIDENT IN MY VOICE, AS IT IS THE SPIRIT OF THE LORD SPEAKING THROUGH ME."

TODAY'S WORD TODAY

BIBLEFY

AMY SHIELS

"I AM CONFIDENT THERE IS NOTHING COVERED THAT SHALL NOT BE REVEALED."

TODAY'S WORD TODAY

BIBLEFY

AMY SHIELS

JULY 13 2025

"I LOVE THE LORD WITH ALL MY HEART, SOUL, AND STRENGTH, AND SHALL LOVE OTHERS AS MYSELF."

TODAY'S WORD TODAY

BIBLEFY

AMY SHIELS

JULY 14 2025

"I IMPROVE MY LIFE WITH HARD WORK."

TODAY'S WORD TODAY

BIBLEFY

AMY SHIELS

JULY 15 2025

"I CONFESS, PETITION, AND PRAISE THROUGH MY PRAYERS."

TODAY'S WORD TODAY

JULY 16 2025

"GUIDE ME IN YOUR WISDOM, DEAR GOD. ASSIST ME IN BECOMING A BETTER PERSON."

TODAY'S WORD TODAY

BIBLEFY

AMY SHIELS

"LORD, PLEASE GIVE ME REST WHEN IT'S NEEDED."

TODAY'S WORD TODAY

JULY 18 2025

"I FOLLOW HIS GUIDANCE; THEREFORE I AM SAFEGUARDED."

TODAY'S WORD TODAY

BIBLEFY

AMY SHIELS

"I BELIEVE IN HIS MIRACULOUS POWERS."

TODAY'S WORD TODAY

BIBLEFY

AMY SHIELS

JULY 20 2025

"I AM PERFECT IN JESUS CHRIST."

TODAY'S WORD TODAY

BIBLEFY

AMY SHIELS

JULY 21 2025

"I AM BRAVE, I STAND STRONG, AND BELIEVE THE POWER OF JESUS."

TODAY'S WORD TODAY

BIBLEFY

AMY SHIELS

JULY 22 2025

"IN CHRIST, I AM A NEW CREATURE: OLD THINGS ARE GONE; ALL THINGS HAVE BECOME NEW."

TODAY'S WORD TODAY

BIBLEFY

AMY SHIELS

JULY 23 2025

"WITH AN OPEN HEART I TRULY EXPERIENCE THE POWER OF THE LORD."

TODAY'S WORD TODAY

BIBLEFY

AMY SHIELS

JULY 24 2025

"I SEE WITH MY EYES, HEAR WITH MY EARS, UNDERSTAND WITH MY HEART."

TODAY'S WORD TODAY

BIBLEFY

AMY SHIELS

JULY 25 2025

"I AM PERPLEXED, NOT IN DESPAIR; PERSECUTED, NOT FORSAKEN; CAST DOWN, NOT DESTROYED."

TODAY'S WORD TODAY

BIBLEFY

AMY SHIELS

JULY 26 2025

"I AM PATIENT: WHEAT AND WEEDS GROW TOGETHER UNTIL HARVEST; THEN KEEP I THE WHEAT."

TODAY'S WORD TODAY

BIBLEFY

AMY SHIELS

JULY 27 2025

"WHEN I ASK, IT IS GRANTED; WHEN I SEEK, I DISCOVER; I KNOCK, AND THE DOOR IS OPENED FOR ME."

TODAY'S WORD TODAY

BIBLEFY

AMY SHIELS

"I HAVE PATIENCE IN THE PROCESS."

TODAY'S WORD TODAY

BIBLEFY

AMY SHIELS

JULY 29 2025

"WHEN I ASK FOR HIS PRESENCE I AM ALWAYS GUIDED."

TODAY'S WORD TODAY

JULY 30 2025

"THE KINGDOM OF HEAVEN IS LIKE HIDDEN TREASURE: UPON DISCOVERY, I WILL SELL ALL TO OBTAIN IT."

TODAY'S WORD TODAY

BIBLEFY

AMY SHIELS

JULY 31 2025

"ANGELS DISCERN WHAT IS GOOD AND GUIDE US TOWARD HEAVEN."

TODAY'S WORD TODAY

BIBLEFY

AMY SHIELS

AUGUST

TODAY'S WORD TODAY

BIBLEFY

AMY SHIELS

AUGUST 1 2025

"GOD GIFTS MIRACLES WHERE THEY ARE BELIEVED."

TODAY'S WORD TODAY

BIBLEFY

AMY SHIELS

AUGUST 2 2025

"THANK YOU FOR THE COMFORT OF BELIEVING IN YOU LORD."

TODAY'S WORD TODAY

BIBLEFY

AMY SHIELS

AUGUST 3 2025

"I FOCUS MY ATTENTION ON HIGHER ASPIRATIONS."

TODAY'S WORD TODAY

BIBLEFY

AMY SHIELS

AUGUST 4 2025

"IF I HAVE TIME TO COMPLAIN, I USE IT TO TAKE ACTION INSTEAD."

TODAY'S WORD TODAY

BIBLEFY

AMY SHIELS

"I HAVE COURAGE! I AM NOT AFRAID!"

TODAY'S WORD TODAY

BIBLEFY

AMY SHIELS

AUGUST 6 2025

"I FIND REDEMPTION THROUGH MY LOVE FOR GOD."

TODAY'S WORD TODAY

BIBLEFY

AMY SHIELS

AUGUST 7 2025

"I WILL DIG DEEP INTO MY BELIEF AND I WILL FIND A WAY."

TODAY'S WORD TODAY

BIBLEFY

AMY SHIELS

AUGUST 8 2025

"THE LORD GOD IS IN HEAVEN ABOVE AND ON THE EARTH BENEATH: HE IS MY GUIDE."

TODAY'S WORD TODAY

BIBLEFY

AMY SHIELS

AUGUST 9 2025

"I LOVE THE LORD WITH ALL MY HEART, MY SOUL, AND MY STRENGTH."

TODAY'S WORD TODAY

BIBLEFY

AMY SHIELS

AUGUST 10 2025

"I FIGHT THE GOOD FIGHT WITH WORDS."

TODAY'S WORD TODAY

BIBLEFY

AMY SHIELS

AUGUST 11 2025

"HE IS MY PRAISE. HE IS MY LORD."

TODAY'S WORD TODAY

BIBLEFY

AMY SHIELS

AUGUST 12 2025

"THE LORD LEADS THE WAY FOR ME; HE IS BY MY SIDE AND WILL NOT LET ME DOWN."

TODAY'S WORD TODAY

BIBLEFY

AMY SHIELS

AUGUST 13 2025

"I AM NEVER ALONE, GOD IS WITH ME."

TODAY'S WORD TODAY

BIBLEFY

AMY SHIELS

AUGUST 14 2025

"WITHOUT A DOUBT, GOD IS LIVING AMONG US."

TODAY'S WORD TODAY

BIBLEFY

AMY SHIELS

AUGUST 15 2025

"BY GOD'S GRACE, I AM WHO I AM; MY HARD WORK IS EMPOWERED BY HIM."

TODAY'S WORD TODAY

BIBLEFY

AMY SHIELS

AUGUST 16 2025

"I CHOOSE THIS DAY TO SERVE THE LORD."

TODAY'S WORD TODAY

BIBLEFY

AMY SHIELS

AUGUST 17 2025

"I HIDE NOTHING FROM YOU LORD PLEASE GIVE ME YOUR COUNSEL."

TODAY'S WORD TODAY

BIBLEFY

AMY SHIELS

AUGUST 18 2025

"PLEASE SHOW ME WHAT GOOD SHOULD I DO TO HAVE ETERNAL LIFE?"

TODAY'S WORD TODAY

BIBLEFY

AMY SHIELS

AUGUST 19 2025

"AN ANGEL SAYS: THE LORD STANDS WITH THOSE OF VALOR."

TODAY'S WORD TODAY

BIBLEFY

AMY SHIELS

"THOSE WHO BEAR FRUIT FOR OTHERS' CONSUMPTION ARE BLESSED."

TODAY'S WORD TODAY

BIBLEFY

AMY SHIELS

AUGUST 21 2025

"MANY ARE CALLED BUT FEW ARE CHOSEN. MAY GOD CHOOSE ME."

TODAY'S WORD TODAY

BIBLEFY

AMY SHIELS

"I LOVE THE LORD WITH ALL MY HEART, MY SOUL, AND MY MIND."

TODAY'S WORD TODAY

BIBLEFY

AMY SHIELS

AUGUST 23 2025

"MY EYES ARE FIXED ON MY GOAL; I PURSUE IT WITH DETERMINATION."

TODAY'S WORD TODAY

BIBLEFY

AMY SHIELS

AUGUST 24 2025

"THE DOOR TO HEAVEN IS NARROW. I WILL DO MY PART TO GRANT ACCESS."

TODAY'S WORD TODAY

BIBLEFY

AMY SHIELS

AUGUST 25 2025

"I LABOR IN THE NAME OF THE LORD."

TODAY'S WORD TODAY

BIBLEFY

AMY SHIELS

AUGUST 26 2025

"I WORK ON MYSELF THAT I MAY HELP OTHERS."

TODAY'S WORD TODAY

BIBLEFY

AMY SHIELS

AUGUST 27 2025

"I WILL WALK WITH GRACE WORTHY OF GOD'S INVITATION TO THE KINGDOM OF HEAVEN."

TODAY'S WORD TODAY

BIBLEFY

AMY SHIELS

"I EMBRACE LIFE TO THE FULLEST WHEN I REMAIN STEADFAST IN THE LORD."

TODAY'S WORD TODAY

BIBLEFY

AMY SHIELS

AUGUST 29 2025

"GOD HAS CALLED ME INTO HOLINESS AND GIVEN ME HIS HOLY SPIRIT."

TODAY'S WORD TODAY

BIBLEFY

AMY SHIELS

AUGUST 30 2025

"I STUDY TO BE QUIET, TO DO MY OWN BUSINESS, AND TO WORK WITH MY OWN HANDS."

TODAY'S WORD TODAY

BIBLEFY

AMY SHIELS

"I HUMBLE MYSELF TO BE ELEVATED BECAUSE I KNOW WHAT IS RIGHT."

TODAY'S WORD TODAY

BIBLEFY

AMY SHIELS

SEPTEMBER

TODAY'S WORD TODAY

BIBLEFY

AMY SHIELS

SEPTEMBER 1 2025

"SOMETIMES MY GREATEST GIFTS ARE VALUED WHERE I LEAST EXPECT THEM TO BE."

TODAY'S WORD TODAY

BIBLEFY

AMY SHIELS

SEPTEMBER 2 2025

"LET ME NOT BE LIKE OTHERS WHO ARE ASLEEP, BUT LET ME BE AWAKE AND CLEAR MINDED."

TODAY'S WORD TODAY

BIBLEFY

AMY SHIELS

SEPTEMBER 3 2025

"I SEEK OUT THOSE WHO ARE READY TO LISTEN, AND SHARE MY GIFTS WITH THEM."

TODAY'S WORD TODAY

BIBLEFY

AMY SHIELS

SEPTEMBER 4 2025

"I SERVE OTHERS TO FEEL GOD'S GRACE IN MY HEART."

TODAY'S WORD TODAY

BIBLEFY

AMY SHIELS

SEPTEMBER 5 2025

"ALL THINGS WERE CREATED BY HIM. WITH GOD IN MY HEART ALL THINGS HOLD TOGETHER."

TODAY'S WORD TODAY

BIBLEFY

AMY SHIELS

SEPTEMBER 6 2025

"I CONTINUE MY FAITH, GROUNDED AND SETTLED BECAUSE YOU HAVE BLESSED ME, FATHER."

TODAY'S WORD TODAY

BIBLEFY

AMY SHIELS

SEPTEMBER 7 2025

"THE LORD SERVES AS MY SHIELD; HE IS MY GLORY AND THE ONE WHO LIFTS MY HEAD HIGH."

TODAY'S WORD TODAY

BIBLEFY

AMY SHIELS

SEPTEMBER 8 2025

"I THRIVE IN THE LORD'S POWER AND GLORY!"

TODAY'S WORD TODAY

BIBLEFY

AMY SHIELS

SEPTEMBER 9 2025

"MY FAITH IS STRONG, SO I WALK WITH CONFIDENCE."

TODAY'S WORD TODAY

BIBLEFY

AMY SHIELS

SEPTEMBER 10 2025

"I CELEBRATE THE DAY AND REJOICE; HIS DEDICATION BRINGS GREAT REWARDS."

TODAY'S WORD TODAY

BIBLEFY

AMY SHIELS

SEPTEMBER 11 2025

"I PRAY FOR THOSE WHO HAVE WRONGED ME, FOR THIS MY REWARD WILL BE GREAT."

TODAY'S WORD TODAY

BIBLEFY

AMY SHIELS

SEPTEMBER 12 2025

"I AM SWIFT TO FORGIVE AND SLOW TO PASS JUDGMENT."

TODAY'S WORD TODAY

SEPTEMBER 13 2025

"OUR WORDS REFLECT THE FULLNESS OF OUR HEARTS. I LISTEN TO THOSE WHO POSSESS A KIND HEART."

TODAY'S WORD TODAY

BIBLEFY

AMY SHIELS

SEPTEMBER 14 2025

"THANK YOU LORD FOR ALL YOU HAVE GIVEN US!"

TODAY'S WORD TODAY

BIBLEFY

AMY SHIELS

SEPTEMBER 15 2025

"I WILL BE DISCREET WHEN OFFERING HELP."

TODAY'S WORD TODAY

BIBLEFY

AMY SHIELS

SEPTEMBER 16 2025

"I TEND TO MY HOME BEFORE TENDING TO ANOTHER'S."

BIBLEFY

AMY SHIELS

SEPTEMBER 17 2025

"I BELIEVE IN THE MYSTERY OF FAITH. I BELIEVE THE WORLD IS GOOD."

TODAY'S WORD TODAY

BIBLEFY

AMY SHIELS

SEPTEMBER 18 2025

"FORGIVE THOSE YOU LOVE; THE ONE WHO IS NOT FORGIVEN GIVES NOTHING IN RETURN."

TODAY'S WORD TODAY

BIBLEFY

AMY SHIELS

"I STAND STRONG IN GOD'S WORD."

TODAY'S WORD TODAY

BIBLEFY

AMY SHIELS

SEPTEMBER 20 2025

"THOSE WHO, WITH AN HONEST AND SINCERE HEART, HEAR THE WORD AND RETAIN IT."

TODAY'S WORD TODAY

BIBLEFY

AMY SHIELS

SEPTEMBER 21 2025

"I PRAY AND BELIEVE WITHOUT DOUBT."

TODAY'S WORD TODAY

BIBLEFY

AMY SHIELS

"HELP OTHERS WHEN YOU KNOW YOU CAN."

TODAY'S WORD TODAY

BIBLEFY

AMY SHIELS

SEPTEMBER 23 2025

"WHEN I CAN DO GOOD, I DO IT WITHOUT HASTE."

TODAY'S WORD TODAY

BIBLEFY

AMY SHIELS

"DEAR GOD, GIVE ME SANCTUARY AND BUILD A WALL OF PEACE AROUND ME."

TODAY'S WORD TODAY

BIBLEFY

AMY SHIELS

SEPTEMBER 25 2025

"IF YOU ARE NOT WELCOMED BY SOMEONE, SHAKE OFF THEIR NEGATIVITY AND SHINE BRIGHT ELSEWHERE."

TODAY'S WORD TODAY

BIBLEFY

AMY SHIELS

SEPTEMBER 26 2025

"I AM STRONG, FOR HE IS WITH ME ALWAYS."

TODAY'S WORD TODAY

BIBLEFY

AMY SHIELS

SEPTEMBER 27 2025

"GOD, YOUR BLESSINGS ARE ENDLESS AND CONTINUALLY AMAZE ME. THANK YOU FOR YOUR GIFTS."

TODAY'S WORD TODAY

BIBLEFY

AMY SHIELS

"THE BLESSED UPHOLD FAITH, ENSURE JUSTICE FOR THE OPPRESSED, AND SHARE FOOD WITH THE HUNGRY."

TODAY'S WORD TODAY

BIBLEFY

AMY SHIELS

SEPTEMBER 29 2025

"GOODNESS CAN NEVER BE DESTROYED."

TODAY'S WORD TODAY

BIBLEFY

AMY SHIELS

SEPTEMBER 30 2025

"THIS TOO SHALL PASS."

TODAY'S WORD TODAY

BIBLEFY

AMY SHIELS

OCTOBER

TODAY'S WORD TODAY

BIBLEFY

AMY SHIELS

OCTOBER 1 2025

"LORD, I SHALL FOLLOW YOU WHEREVER YOU SHALL GO."

TODAY'S WORD TODAY

BIBLEFY

AMY SHIELS

OCTOBER 2 2025

"LORD, I KNOW I HAVE A LOT TO LEARN. PLEASE GUIDE ME."

TODAY'S WORD TODAY

BIBLEFY

AMY SHIELS

OCTOBER 3 2025

"I AM FOR A PEACEFUL WORLD AND SHALL DO MY PART TO PROTECT US."

TODAY'S WORD TODAY

BIBLEFY

AMY SHIELS

OCTOBER 4 2025

"GOD IS MY PROTECTOR I AM SAFE."

TODAY'S WORD TODAY

BIBLEFY

AMY SHIELS

"THE LORD IS MY FATHER; I AM HIS CHILD."

TODAY'S WORD TODAY

BIBLEFY

AMY SHIELS

OCTOBER 6 2025

"I LOVE THE LORD WITH MY HEART AND SOUL. I SHARE THAT LOVE WITH THOSE AROUND ME."

TODAY'S WORD TODAY

BIBLEFY

AMY SHIELS

OCTOBER 7 2025

"MY GOODNESS CANNOT BE TAKEN FROM ME."

TODAY'S WORD TODAY

BIBLEFY

AMY SHIELS

OCTOBER 8 2025

"GOD, FORGIVE US OUR SINS AND GUIDE US TO TRUTHFULNESS."

TODAY'S WORD TODAY

BIBLEFY

AMY SHIELS

OCTOBER 9 2025

"I SERVE GOD BECAUSE IT MAKES ME JOYFUL."

TODAY'S WORD TODAY

BIBLEFY

AMY SHIELS

OCTOBER 10 2025

"I FORGIVE EVERYONE WHO IS INDEBTED TO ME."

TODAY'S WORD TODAY

BIBLEFY

AMY SHIELS

OCTOBER 11 2025

"BLESSED ARE THOSE WHO KEEP THE WORD OF THE LORD."

TODAY'S WORD TODAY

BIBLEFY

AMY SHIELS

OCTOBER 12 2025

"I BELIEVE IN THE LORD OUR GOD, AND HE BELIEVES IN ME."

TODAY'S WORD TODAY

BIBLEFY

AMY SHIELS

OCTOBER 13 2025

"GOD GIVES ME GRACE FOR MY OBEDIENCE TO FAITH."

TODAY'S WORD TODAY

BIBLEFY

AMY SHIELS

OCTOBER 14 2025

"GOD HAS GIVEN ME THE TOOLS I NEED TO SUCCEED."

TODAY'S WORD TODAY

BIBLEFY

AMY SHIELS

OCTOBER 15 2025

"AT WHATEVER POINT I JUDGE ANOTHER I AM CONDEMNING MYSELF."

TODAY'S WORD TODAY

BIBLEFY

AMY SHIELS

OCTOBER 16 2025

"WE ARE EVERY ONE OF US SINNERS. I WILL DO BETTER."

TODAY'S WORD TODAY

BIBLEFY

AMY SHIELS

"NOTHING THAT IS HIDDEN SHALL NOT BE KNOWN. BE HONEST."

TODAY'S WORD TODAY

BIBLEFY

AMY SHIELS

OCTOBER 18 2025

"THE LORD STANDS WITH ME AND STRENGTHENS ME."

TODAY'S WORD TODAY

BIBLEFY

AMY SHIELS

OCTOBER 19 2025

"WE MUST ALWAYS PRAY AND NOT SHY AWAY FROM OUR DUTY."

TODAY'S WORD TODAY

BIBLEFY

AMY SHIELS

OCTOBER 20 2025

"A PERSON'S LIFE IS NOT DEFINED BY WHAT THE PERSON POSSESSES. DEFINE FOR YOURSELF."

TODAY'S WORD TODAY

BIBLEFY

AMY SHIELS

OCTOBER 21 2025

"THROUGH ONE MAN'S OBEDIENCE, MANY WILL BE MADE RIGHTEOUS."

TODAY'S WORD TODAY

BIBLEFY

AMY SHIELS

"I DO THE RIGHT THING EVEN WHEN NO ONE IS WATCHING. I HAVE INTEGRITY."

TODAY'S WORD TODAY

BIBLEFY

AMY SHIELS

OCTOBER 23 2025

"I AM GOOD, FOR THE GIFT FROM GOD IS ETERNAL LIFE."

TODAY'S WORD TODAY

BIBLEFY

AMY SHIELS

OCTOBER 24 2025

"I DELIGHT IN THE LAW OF GOD AND THANK HIM."

TODAY'S WORD TODAY

BIBLEFY

AMY SHIELS

OCTOBER 25 2025

"I AM TRULY SORRY FOR THE WRONGS I HAVE DONE AND AM DEVOTED TO RECONCILING."

TODAY'S WORD TODAY

BIBLEFY

AMY SHIELS

OCTOBER 26 2025

"GIVE GENEROUSLY TO THE MOST HIGH, AND HE WILL REPAY SEVENFOLD."

TODAY'S WORD TODAY

BIBLEFY

AMY SHIELS

OCTOBER 27 2025

"AS LONG AS I AM LED BY THE SPIRIT OF GOD I AM A CHILD OF GOD."

TODAY'S WORD TODAY

BIBLEFY

AMY SHIELS

OCTOBER 28 2025

"HE IS MY REFUGE, HE IS MY FORTRESS; IN THE LORD I TRUST."

TODAY'S WORD TODAY

BIBLEFY

AMY SHIELS

OCTOBER 29 2025

"I STRIVE TO ENTER IN THE NARROW GATES OF HEAVEN, FOR I KNOW MANY SHALL NOT BE ABLE."

TODAY'S WORD TODAY

BIBLEFY

AMY SHIELS

OCTOBER 30 2025

"IF GOD IS FOR US, NO ONE CAN BE AGAINST US."

TODAY'S WORD TODAY

BIBLEFY

AMY SHIELS

OCTOBER 31 2025

"IT IS OUR DUTY TO ASSIST OTHERS; THERE ARE NO JUSTIFICATIONS FOR INACTION."

TODAY'S WORD TODAY

BIBLEFY

AMY SHIELS

NOVEMBER

TODAY'S WORD TODAY

BIBLEFY

AMY SHIELS

"I LIVE IN HARMONY AMONG THE EARTH, THE SEA, AND THE TREES"

TODAY'S WORD TODAY

BIBLEFY

AMY SHIELS

"I BELIEVE IN MY FAITH, FOR IT WOULD BE FOOLISH TO THINK OTHERWISE."

TODAY'S WORD TODAY

BIBLEFY

AMY SHIELS

"BEHOLD THE GOODNESS OF GOD. I SHALL WALK IN HIS PATH AND SPREAD JOY."

TODAY'S WORD TODAY

BIBLEFY

AMY SHIELS

NOVEMBER 4 2025

"GOD, YOU ARE WITH ME ALWAYS. ALL THAT I HAVE IS YOURS."

TODAY'S WORD TODAY

BIBLEFY

AMY SHIELS

"OWE NO MAN ANY THING BUT TO LOVE ONE ANOTHER."

TODAY'S WORD TODAY

BIBLEFY

AMY SHIELS

NOVEMBER 6 2025

"I DON'T LIVE FOR MYSELF - I LIVE FOR THE LORD."

TODAY'S WORD TODAY

BIBLEFY

AMY SHIELS

NOVEMBER 7 2025

"GRACE IS GIVEN TO ME THROUGH GOD THAT I MAY BE FILLED WITH GOODNESS AND KNOWLEDGE."

TODAY'S WORD TODAY

BIBLEFY

AMY SHIELS

NOVEMBER 8 2025

"I EXPRESS MY GRATITUDE TO THOSE WHO HAVE RISKED THEIR OWN LIVES FOR MINE."

TODAY'S WORD TODAY

BIBLEFY

AMY SHIELS

"MY LIFE IS FRUITFUL AND FULL OF JOY."

TODAY'S WORD TODAY

BIBLEFY

AMY SHIELS

NOVEMBER 10 2025

"MY FAITH HAS MADE ME WHOLE."

TODAY'S WORD TODAY

BIBLEFY

AMY SHIELS

NOVEMBER 11 2025

"A RIGHTOUS MIND IS A PEACFUL MIND."

TODAY'S WORD TODAY

BIBLEFY

AMY SHIELS

NOVEMBER 12 2025

"I WILL GAIN WISDOM AND NOT FALL AWAY."

TODAY'S WORD TODAY

BIBLEFY

AMY SHIELS

NOVEMBER 13 2025

"WHEN I TAKE TIME TO LOOK AROUND I SEE THAT I AM SURROUNDED BY HIS GIFTS."

TODAY'S WORD TODAY

BIBLEFY

AMY SHIELS

NOVEMBER 14 2025

"HE HAS GIVEN ME THE POWER TO INVESTIGATE THE WORLD THAT I MAY SEE HOW BEAUTIFUL IT IS."

TODAY'S WORD TODAY

BIBLEFY

AMY SHIELS

NOVEMBER 15 2025

"MAY WE ALL GAZE UPON THE MARVELOUS WONDERS THE LORD HAS CREATED."

TODAY'S WORD TODAY

BIBLEFY

AMY SHIELS

NOVEMBER 16 2025

"FOR THOSE WHO HAVE FAITH WILL GO OUT HAPPILY LEAPING LIKE CALVES FROM THE STALL."

TODAY'S WORD TODAY

BIBLEFY

AMY SHIELS

NOVEMBER 17 2025

"GOD HAS GIVEN ME THE GIFT OF SIGHT TO SEE SUCH BEAUTIFUL THINGS."

TODAY'S WORD TODAY

BIBLEFY

AMY SHIELS

NOVEMBER 18 2025

"GOD COMES TO SAVE THOSE WHO ARE LOST."

TODAY'S WORD TODAY

BIBLEFY

AMY SHIELS

NOVEMBER 19 2025

"I AM PATIENT AND FAITHFUL TO THE LORD; HIS TIMELINE IS PERFECT."

TODAY'S WORD TODAY

BIBLEFY

AMY SHIELS

"EVERY PERSON I SEE HAS THE POTENTIAL TO BE AN ANGEL."

TODAY'S WORD TODAY

BIBLEFY

AMY SHIELS

NOVEMBER 21 2025

"SEE? WE ARE FREE. LET US CELEBRATE!"

TODAY'S WORD TODAY

BIBLEFY

AMY SHIELS

NOVEMBER 22 2025

"I WILL SLEEP AND BUILD COURAGE."

TODAY'S WORD TODAY

BIBLEFY

AMY SHIELS

NOVEMBER 23 2025

"TODAY AND EVERYDAY I AM IN PARADISE WITH THE LORD."

TODAY'S WORD TODAY

BIBLEFY

AMY SHIELS

NOVEMBER 24 2025

"GOD GRANTS ME THE KNOWLEDGE AND SKILLS NECESSARY TO BETTER MYSELF."

TODAY'S WORD TODAY

BIBLEFY

AMY SHIELS

"THE DREAM IS CERTAIN. GOD DELIVERS ON HIS PROMISES."

TODAY'S WORD TODAY

AMY SHIELS

NOVEMBER 26 2025

"I WILL NOT PERISH - PATIENCE WILL GOVERN MY SPIRIT."

TODAY'S WORD TODAY

BIBLEFY

AMY SHIELS

NOVEMBER 27 2025

"I SEE SIGNS IN THE SUN AND THE STARS AND THE MOON. THE SEAS AND THE WAVES INSPIRE ME."

TODAY'S WORD TODAY

BIBLEFY

AMY SHIELS

NOVEMBER 28 2025

"HEAVEN AND EARTH SHALL PASS AWAY, BUT OUR LOVE SHALL REMAIN FOREVER."

TODAY'S WORD TODAY

BIBLEFY

AMY SHIELS

NOVEMBER 29 2025

"I BEHAVE IN SUCH A WAY THAT WHEN THE TIME COMES I WILL BE WORTHY OF MY PLACE IN HEAVEN."

TODAY'S WORD TODAY

BIBLEFY

AMY SHIELS

NOVEMBER 30 2025

"TODAY I CAST OFF THE WORKS OF DARKNESS, AND PUT ON THE ARMOR OF LIGHT."

TODAY'S WORD TODAY

BIBLEFY
AMY SHIELS

DECEMBER

TODAY'S WORD TODAY

BIBLEFY

AMY SHIELS

DECEMBER 1 2025

"MY FAITH IS MY REFUGE. THE LORD LOVES ME AND KEEPS ME STRONG."

TODAY'S WORD TODAY

BIBLEFY

AMY SHIELS

DECEMBER 2 2025

"BLESSED AM I TO SEE THE THINGS THAT I SEE."

TODAY'S WORD TODAY

BIBLEFY

AMY SHIELS

DECEMBER 3 2025

"THE LORD GIFTS US A FEAST OF FAT THINGS: BEAUTY, AND LOVE, AND LIFE IN ABUNDANCE."

TODAY'S WORD TODAY

BIBLEFY

DECEMBER 4 2025

"I TRUST IN THE LORD'S EVERLASTING STRENGTH. HE KEEPS ME IN PERFECT PEACE."

TODAY'S WORD TODAY

BIBLEFY

AMY SHIELS

DECEMBER 5 2025

"I DON'T COMPLAIN BECAUSE WHEN I STAY IN GOOD SPIRIT I GAIN UNDERSTANDING."

TODAY'S WORD TODAY

BIBLEFY

AMY SHIELS

DECEMBER 6 2025

"WHEN HE HEARS MY CRY HE ANSWERS ME."

TODAY'S WORD TODAY

BIBLEFY

AMY SHIELS

DECEMBER 7 2025

"THE SPIRIT OF THE LORD RESTS UPON ME: WISDOM, UNDERSTANDING AND MIGHT."

TODAY'S WORD TODAY

BIBLEFY

AMY SHIELS

"THERE ARE GIFTS IN THE WIND AND THE RAIN; WATER AND WISDOM."

TODAY'S WORD TODAY

BIBLEFY

AMY SHIELS

DECEMBER 9 2025

"BEHOLD, THE NATIONS OF THE WORLD ARE A DROP IN THE BUCKET WHEN THE KINGDOM OF HEAVEN AWAITS."

TODAY'S WORD TODAY

BIBLEFY

AMY SHIELS

"LORD, PLEASE GIVE ME POWER AND STRENGTH WHEN I FEEL WEAK."

TODAY'S WORD TODAY

BIBLEFY

AMY SHIELS

"THE LORD GOD TELLS ME TO FEAR NOT FOR HE IS HELPING ME."

TODAY'S WORD TODAY

BIBLEFY

AMY SHIELS

DECEMBER 12 2025

"THE LORD WAS RAISED OUT OF HIS HOLY HABITATION TO BRING US JOY AND PROTECTION."

TODAY'S WORD TODAY

DECEMBER 13 2025

"I RISE LIKE A FIRE AND BURN LIKE A TORCH TO WORK WITH THE CHALLENGES LIFE PRESENTS ME."

TODAY'S WORD TODAY

BIBLEFY

AMY SHIELS

DECEMBER 14 2025

"I BLOSSOM ABUNDANTLY AND REJOICE WITH JOY BECAUSE I KNOW GOD LOVES ME."

TODAY'S WORD TODAY

BIBLEFY

AMY SHIELS

DECEMBER 15 2025

"I AM OBEDIENT TO THE LORD AND DO NOT QUESTION HIS WAYS."

TODAY'S WORD TODAY

BIBLEFY

AMY SHIELS

DECEMBER 16 2025

"I SHALL NOT LET MY HANDS BE SLACK. I WILL WORK FOR THE GREATER GOOD."

TODAY'S WORD TODAY

DECEMBER 17 2025

"I EMPLOY YOUR STRENGTH; YOUR EXCELLENCY OF DIGNITY AND POWER, O LORD."

TODAY'S WORD TODAY

BIBLEFY

AMY SHIELS

DECEMBER 18 2025

"BEHOLD THE DAYS TO COME, I SHALL LIVE ON MY OWN LAND."

TODAY'S WORD TODAY

BIBLEFY

AMY SHIELS

"I LIVE WITHOUT FEAR BECAUSE I KNOW MY PRAYER WILL BE HEARD."

TODAY'S WORD TODAY

BIBLEFY

AMY SHIELS

DECEMBER 20 2025

"I LISTEN BECAUSE THE LORD HIMSELF WILL SEND ME A SIGN."

TODAY'S WORD TODAY

BIBLEFY

AMY SHIELS

"GRACE AND PEACE TO ALL FROM GOD OUR FATHER."

TODAY'S WORD TODAY

BIBLEFY

AMY SHIELS

DECEMBER 22 2025

"AS LONG AS I LIVE I LEND MYSELF TO THE LORD."

TODAY'S WORD TODAY

BIBLEFY

AMY SHIELS

"GOD'S GRACE SHINES BRIGHT UPON ME!"

TODAY'S WORD TODAY

BIBLEFY

AMY SHIELS

DECEMBER 24 2025

"I WILL GO AND DO ALL THAT IS IN MY HEART. THE LORD IS WITH ME."

TODAY'S WORD TODAY

BIBLEFY

AMY SHIELS

DECEMBER 25 2025

"I AM A CROWN OF GLORY IN THE HAND OF THE LORD AND HE DELIGHTS IN ME."

TODAY'S WORD TODAY

BIBLEFY

AMY SHIELS

DECEMBER 26 2025

"WITH FAITH AND POWER I WILL SEE MIRACLES HAPPEN."

TODAY'S WORD TODAY

BIBLEFY

AMY SHIELS

DECEMBER 27 2025

"HE IS MY REFUGE AND FORTRESS; IN GOD I TRUST."

TODAY'S WORD TODAY

BIBLEFY

AMY SHIELS

DECEMBER 28 2025

"I HONOR THE LORD; WHEN I PRAY I AM HEARD."

TODAY'S WORD TODAY

BIBLEFY

AMY SHIELS

DECEMBER 29 2025

"BE GENTLE AND LISTEN AND THE THOUGHTS OF MANY HEARTS WILL BE REVEALED"

TODAY'S WORD TODAY

BIBLEFY

AMY SHIELS

DECEMBER 30 2025

"I GROW STRONG IN SPIRIT WITH THE GRACE OF GOD UPON ME."

TODAY'S WORD TODAY

BIBLEFY

AMY SHIELS

DECEMBER 31 2025

"I AM BLESSED BY THE HOLY ONE AND ALREADY KNOW THE TRUTH; IN HIM I AM CHERISHED."

TODAY'S WORD TODAY